My Beloved

Embroidered silk letter keepsake
with antique love letters.

My Beloved

Classic Messages of Love

Edited by Edward Lewis
and Robert Myers

HALLMARK EDITIONS

My Beloved

Victor Hugo to Adele Foucher

. . . My Adele, why is there no word for this but joy? Is it because there is no power in human speech to express such happiness?

The sudden bound from mournful resignation to infinite felicity seemed to upset me. Even now I am still beside myself and sometimes I tremble lest I should suddenly awaken from this dream divine.

Oh, now you are mine! At last you are mine! Soon—in a few months, perhaps, my angel will sleep in my arms, will awaken in my arms, will live there. All my thoughts, all my moments, all my looks, will be for you! My Adele!...

And now you will belong to me! Now I am

called on earth to enjoy celestial felicity. I see you as my young wife, then a young mother, but always the same, always my Adele, as tender, as adored in the chastity of married life as in the virgin days of your first love— Dear Love, answer me—tell me if you can conceive the happiness of love immortal in an eternal union!

Heloise to Abelard

We may write to each other; so innocent a pleasure is not denied us. Let us not lose through negligence the only happiness which is left us, and the only one perhaps which the malice of our enemies can never ravish from us. I shall read that you are my husband and you shall see me sign myself your wife. In spite of all our misfortunes you may be what you please in your letter. Letters were first invented for consoling such solitary wretches as myself. Having lost the substantial pleasures of seeing and possessing you, I shall in some measure compensate this loss by the satisfaction I shall find in your writing. There I shall read your most sacred thoughts; I shall carry them always about with me, I shall kiss them every moment; if you can be capable of any jealousy let it be for the fond caresses I shall bestow upon your letters, and envy only the happiness of those rivals.

HELOISE,
prioress of French religious order.

Alexander Hamilton
to Elizabeth Schuyler

Well, my love, here is the middle of October;
a few weeks more and you are mine; a sweet
reflection to me—is it so to my charmer? Do
you find yourself more or less anxious for the
moment to arrive as it approaches? This is a
good criterion to determine the degree of your
affection by. You have had an age for consideration, time enough for even a woman to
know her mind in. Do you begin to repent or
not? Remember you are going to do a very
serious thing. For though our sex have gen-
erously given up a part of its prerogatives, and
husbands have no longer the power of life and
death, as the wiser husbands of former days
had, yet we still retain the power of happiness
and misery; and if you are prudent you will
not trust the felicity of your future life to one
in whom you have not good reason for implicit
confidence . . .

I stopped to read over my letter—it is a

9

motley mixture of fond extravagance and sprightly dullness: the truth is I am too much in love to be either reasonable or witty: I feel in the extreme; and when I attempt to speak of my feelings I rave. I have remarked to you before that real tenderness has also a tincture of sadness, and when I affect the lively my melting heart rebels. It is separated from you and it cannot be cheerful. Love is a sort of insanity and everything I write savors strongly of it; that you return it is the best proof of your madness also. I tell you, my Betsy, you are negligent; you do not write me often enough. Take more care of my happiness, for there is nothing your Hamilton would not do to promote yours.

Henriette to Casanova

I have been forced to leave you, my only friend, but do not add to your grief by thinking of mine. Let us not waste time deploring our fate, let us rather imagine we have had an agreeable dream, and surely never did dream so delicious last so long! We can boast that we were perfectly happy for three whole months; how many mortals can say as much? Let us

GIOVANNI JACOPO CASANOVA,
Italian adventurer.

not forget each other, though we must never
meet again. I know it will please you to hear
that I have put my affairs in order, and that
for the rest of my life I shall be as happy as it
is possible for me to be, away from you. I do
not even know who you are, but there is no
one in the world so familiar with your every
thought as I am. I shall never have another
lover in my life, but in this you must not imi-
tate me. I hope that you will love again, and
that your good genius will help you to find
another Henriette. *Adieu, adieu.*

Lord Byron to Contessa Guiccioli

You sometimes tell me that I have been your *first* real love—and I assure you that you shall be my last Passion. I may well hope not to fall in love again, now that everything has become indifferent to me. Before I knew you—I felt an interest in many women, but never in one only. Now I love *you*, there is no other woman in the world for me.

You talk of tears and of our unhappiness; my sorrow is within; I do not weep. You have fastened on your arm a likeness that does not deserve so highly; but yours is in my heart, it has become part of my life, of my soul; and were there another life after this one, there too you would be mine—without you where would Paradise be . . .?

My sweetest treasure—I am trembling as I write to you, as I trembled when I saw you— but no longer—with such sweet heartbeats. I have a thousand things to say to you—and, alas, how many Sighs! Love me—not as I love you—for that would make you too unhappy, love me not as I deserve, for that would be too little—but as your Heart commands. Do not doubt me—I am and always shall be your most tender lover.

P.S. How much happier than I is this letter: which in a few days will be in your hands— and perhaps may even be brought to your lips. With such a hope I am kissing it before it goes. Goodbye—my soul.

GEORGE GORDON, LORD BYRON,
English poet, after a portrait by Thomas Phillips.

John Keats to Fanny Brawne

I see life in nothing but the certainty of your Love—convince me of it my sweetest. If I am not somehow convinced I shall die of agony. If we love we must not live as other men and women do—I cannot brook the wolfsbane of fashion and foppery and tattle. You must be mine to die upon the rack if I want you. I do not pretend to say I have more feeling than my fellows—but I wish you seriously to look over my letters kind and unkind and consider whether the Person who wrote them can be able to endure much longer the agonies and uncertainties which you are so peculiarly made to create—My recovery of bodily health will be of no benefit to me if you are not all mine when I am well. For God's sake save me—or tell me my passion is of too awful a nature for you. Again God bless you.

Robert Burns to Agnes M'Lehose

. . . Will you open, with satisfaction and delight, a letter from a man who loves you, who has loved you, and who will love you to death, through death, and for ever? Oh, Clarinda!

ROBERT BURNS,
Scottish poet, in a contemporary silhouette.

what do I owe to Heaven for blessing me with
such a piece of exalted excellence as you! I
call over your idea, as a miser counts over his
treasure. Tell me, were you studious to please
me last night? I am sure you did it to trans-
port. How rich am I who have such a treasure
as you . . .!

Tomorrow night, according to your own di-
rection, I shall watch the window: 'tis the star
that guides me to paradise . . . .

Samuel Coleridge to Mary Evans

Too long has my heart been the torture house
of suspense. After infinite struggles of irresolu-
tion, I will at last dare to request of you, Mary,
that you will communicate to me whether or
no you are engaged to Mr. _____. I conjure
you not to consider this request as presump-
tious indelicacy. Upon mine honour, I have
made it with no other design or expectation

than that of arming my fortitude by total hope-lessness. Read this letter with benevolence—and consign it to oblivion.

For four years I have *endeavoured* to smother a very ardent attachment; in what degree I have succeeded you must know better than I can. With quick perceptions of moral beauty, it was impossible for me not to admire in you your sensibility regulated by judgment, your gaity proceeding from a cheerful heart acting on the stores of a strong understanding. At first I voluntarily invited the recollection of these qualities into my mind. I made them the perpetual object of my reveries, yet I entertained no one sentiment beyond that of the immediate pleasure annexed to the thinking of you. At length it became a habit. I awoke from the delusion, and found that I had unwittingly harboured a passion which I felt neither the power nor the courage to subdue. My associations were irrevocably formed, and your image was blended with every idea. I thought of you incessantly; yet the spirit (if spirit there be that condescends to record the lonely beatings of my heart), that spirit knows that I thought of you with the purity of a brother. Happy were I, had it been with no more than a brother's ardour!

Bismark to Johanna

. . . We ought to share with each other joy and suffering—I your suffering and you mine; that we are not united for the sake of showing and sharing with each other only that which gives pleasure; but that you may pour out your heart at all times to me and I to you, whatever it may contain; that I must and will bear your sorrows, your thoughts, your naughtinesses, if you have any, and love you as you are—not as

you ought to be or might be. Make me service-
able, use me for what purpose you will, ill-
treat me without and within, if you have the
wish to do so. I am there for that purpose, at
your disposal; but never be embarrassed in
any way with me. Trust me unreservedly, in
the conviction that I accept everything that
comes from you with profound love, whether
it be glad or patient. Do not keep your gloomy
thoughts for yourself while you look on me
with cheerful brow and merry eyes, but share
with me in word and look what you have in
your heart, whether it be blessing or sorrow.

Sir Richard Steele to Mary Scurlock

I writ you on Saturday, by Mrs. Warren, and
give you this trouble to urge the same request
I made then; which was, that I may be ad-
mitted to wait upon you. I should be very far
from desiring this if it were a transgression of
the most severe rules to allow it. I know you
are very much above the little arts which are
frequent in your sex, of giving unnecessary
torment to their admirers; I therefore hope
you will do so much justice to the generous

passion I have for you, as to let me have an opportunity of acquainting you upon what motives I pretend to your good opinion. I shall not trouble you with my sentiments till I know how they will be received; and as I know no reason why the difference of sex should make our language to each other differ from the ordinary rules of right reason, I shall affect plainness and sincerity in my discourse to you, as much as other lovers do perplexity and rapture. Instead of saying 'I shall die for you', I profess I should be glad to lead my life with you. You are as beautiful, as witty, as prudent, and as good-humoured as any woman breathing; but, I must confess to you, I regard all these excellences as you will please to direct them for my happiness or misery. With me, madam, the only lasting motive to love, is the hope of its becoming mutual. I beg of you to let Mrs. Warren send me word when I may attend you. I promise you, I will talk of nothing but indifferent things; though, at the same time, I know not how I shall approach you in the tender moment of first seeing you after this declaration which has been made by, madam,

Your most obedient and most faithful humble servant.

THE BELLE'S COMPLETE LETTER WRITER *supplied sentiments for 19th century love letters.*

Beethoven to His Immortal Beloved

Oh, God! look out into the beauties of nature
and comfort yourself with that which must be
—love demands everything and that very just-
ly—thus it is with me so far as you are con-
cerned, and you with me. If we were wholly
united you would feel the pain of it as little
as I . . . We shall soon surely see each other;
moreover, I cannot communicate to you the
observations I have made during the last few

22

days touching my own life—if our hearts were always close together I would make none of the kind. My heart is full of many things to say to you—Ah!—there are moments when I feel that speech is nothing after all—cheer up —remain my true, my only treasure, my all as I am yours; the gods must send us the rest that which shall be best for us.

Elizabeth Barrett to Robert Browning

Best and kindest of all that ever were to be loved in dreams, and wondered at and loved out of them, you are indeed! I cannot make you feel how I felt that night when I knew that to save me an anxious thought you had come so far so late—it was almost too much to feel, and it is too much to speak. So let it pass. You will never act so again, ever dearest— you shall not. If the post sins, why leave the sin to the post; and I will remember for the future, will be ready to remember, how post- men are fallible and how you live at the end of a lane—and not be uneasy about a silence if there should be one unaccounted for. For the Tuesday coming, I shall remember that too—who could forget it? I put it in the niche of the wall, one golden lamp more of your giving, to throw light purely down to the end of my life . . . .

John Jay Chapman to His Wife

. . .This is a love letter, is it not? How long is it since I have written you a love letter, my love, my Minna? Was the spring hidden that now comes bubbling up overflowing curb and coping-stone, washing my feet and my knees and my whole self? How are the waters of the world sweet—if we should die, we have drunk them. If we should sin—or separate—if we should fail or secede—we have tasted of happiness—we must be written in the book of the blessed. We have had what life could give, we have eaten of the tree of knowledge, we have known—we have been the mystery of the universe.

Is love a hand or a foot—is it a picture or a poem or a fireside—is it a compact or a permission or eagles that meet in the clouds—No, no, no, no. It is light and heat and hand and foot and ego. If I take the wings of the morning and remain in the uttermost parts of the sea, there art thou also—He descended into

24

Hell and on the third day róse again—and there art thou also—in the lust or business—in the stumbling and dry places, in sickness and health—every sort of sickness there also—what matter is it what else the world contains—if you only are in it in every part of it? I can find no corner of it without you—my eyes would not see it. It is empty—I have seen all that is there and it is nothing, and over creation are your wings . . . .

Henry VIII to Anne Boleyn

Myne awne Sweetheart, this shall be to advertise you of the great ellingness* that I find here since your departing, for I ensure you, me thinketh the Tyme longer since your departing now last than I was wont to do a whole Fortnight; I think your Kindness and my Fervence of Love causeth it, for otherwise I wolde

*loneliness

HENRY VIII, *King of England,*
after the famous painting by Hans Holbein.

not thought it possible, that for so little a while it should have grieved me, but now that I am comeing toward you, me thinketh my Pains by half released, and also I am right well comforted, insomuch that my Book maketh substantially for my Matter, in writing whereof I have spent above IIII Hours this Day, which caused me now write the shorter Letter to you at this Tyme, because of some Payne in my Head, wishing my self (specially an Evening) in my Sweethearts Armes whose pritty Lips I trust shortly to kysse. Writne with the Hand of him that was, is, and shall be yours by his will . . . .

James Thomson to Miss Young

After a disagreeable stage-coach journey, disagreeable in itself, and infinitely so as it carried me from you, I am come to the most agreeable place and company in the world. The park, where we pass a great part of our time, is thoroughly delightful, quite enchanting. It consists of several little hills, finely tufted with wood, and rising softly one above another; from which are seen a great variety of at once beautiful and grand extensive prospects: but

I am most charmed with its sweet embowered retirements, and particularly with a winding dale that runs through the middle of it. This dale is overhung with deep woods, and enlivened by a stream, that, now gushing from mossy rocks, now falling in cascades, and now spreading into a calm length of water, forms the most natural and pleasing scene imaginable. At the source of this water, composed of some pretty rills, that purl from beneath the roots of oaks, there is as fine a retired seat, as lover's heart could wish. There I often sit, and with a dear exquisite mixture of pleasure and pain of all that love can boast of excellent and tender, think of you. But what do I talk of sitting and thinking of you there? wherever I am, and however employed, I never cease to think of my loveliest Miss Young. You are part of my being; you mix with all my thoughts, even the most studious, and instead of disturbing give them greater harmony and spirit. Ah tell me, do I not now and then steal a tender thought from you? I may claim that distinction from the merit of my love. Yes, I love you to that degree as must inspire into the coldest breast a mutual passion. So look to your heart, for you will scarce be able to defend it against my tenderness.

William Makepeace Thackeray
to Isabella Shawe

My love for you is greater than I thought, for it has withstood this terrible three days trial. I have tried to leave you, & you will hardly credit me that I felt obliged to return—for I do not believe in spite of all this heartlessness on your part, that you ever can be other than my wife—You may recollect, that after our second quarrel, we made a kind of vow that, happen what would—you & I were bound together & married before God, & that I told you but a few nights since, that I had prayed to Him to give me aid in quelling any improper desires which might create your disgust or lessen me in your esteem . . . .

However, take me or leave me—I never can love you as I have; although you fancy that my love for you was not 'pure' enough—it was a love of which any woman in the world should have been proud, and which I never can give to any other—but still, dearest, I love you; forgive me my trespasses as I here remit you yours, and you will restore happiness to your family, & to one whose misery you never can feel or know, please God.

Madame Du Barry
Replies to King Louis XV

The billet traced by your noble hands renders me the happiest of women. My joy is beyond description. Thanks, monsieur le Baron, for your charming flowers. Alas! they will be faded and withered by to-morrow, but not so fleeting and short-lived are the sentiments with which you have inspired me. Believe me, the desire you express to see me again is entirely mutual; and in the impatience with which you await

MADAME DU BARRY,
mistress of King Louis XV of France,
after a painting by Drovais.

our next interview, I read but my own sentiments. The ardor with which you long to em-
brace me, is fully equalled by the affection
which leads me to desire no gratification greater
than that of passing my whole life in your
society . . . .

Voltaire to Olympe Dunoyer

From Prison

I am a prisoner here in the name of the King;
they can take my life, but not the love that I
feel for you. Yes, my adorable mistress, to-
night I shall see you, and if I had to put my
head on the block to do it. For Heaven's sake,
do not speak to me in such disastrous terms as
you write; you must live and be cautious; beware of madame your mother as of your worst
enemy. What do I say? Beware of everybody,
trust no one; keep yourself in readiness, as
soon as the moon is visible; I shall leave the
hotel incognito, take a carriage or a chaise, we
shall drive like the wind to Scheveningen; I
shall take paper and ink with me; we shall
write our letters.

If you love me, reassure yourself, and call

all your strength and presence of mind to your aid; do not let your mother notice anything, try to have your picture, and be assured that the menace of the greatest tortures will not prevent me to serve you.

No, nothing has the power to part me from you; our love is based upon virtue, and will last as long as our lives. *Adieu,* there is nothing that I will not brave for your sake; you deserve much more than that. *Adieu,* my dear heart!

Shelley to His Friend, Gisborne

What is Love?

We are born into the world, and there is something within us which, from the instant that we live, more and more thirsts after its likeness . . . , the meeting with an understanding capable of clearly estimating our own; an imagination which should enter into and seize upon the subtle and delicate peculiarities which we have delighted to cherish and unfold in

Elegant lady of the 19th century court in evening dress.

secret; with a frame whose nerves, like the chords of two exquisite lyres, strung to the accompaniment of one delightful voice, vibrate with the vibrations of our own; and of a combination of all these in such proportion as the type within demands; this is the invisible and unattainable point to which love tends; and to attain which, it urges forth the powers of man to arrest the faintest shadow of that without the possession of which there is no rest nor respite to the heart over which it rules.

Napoleon to Josephine

I don't love you, not at all; on the contrary, I detest you—You're a naughty, gawky, foolish Cinderella. You never write me; you don't love your husband, you know what pleasure your letters give him, and yet you haven't written him six lines, dashed off casually!

What do you do all day, Madam? What is the affair so important as to leave you no time to write to your devoted lover? What affection stifles and puts to one side the love, the tender and constant love you promised him? Of what sort can be that marvelous being, that new lover who absorbs every moment, tyrannizes over your days, and prevents your giving any attention to your husband? Josephine, take care! Some fine night, the doors will be broken open, and there I'll be.

Indeed, I am very uneasy, my love, at receiving no news of you; write me quickly four pages, pages full of agreeable things which shall fill my heart with the pleasantest feelings.

I hope before long to crush you in my arms and cover you with a million kisses burning as though beneath the equator.

. . . When I see and believe your attachment for me, do you think that any cause in the world could render it less a source of joy to me? I mean as far as I myself am considered. Now

"Heartsick": late 18th century silhouette,
a popular form of letter decoration.

36

if you ever fancy that I am vain of your love
for me, you will be unjust, remember. If it
were less dear, and less above me, I might be
vain perhaps. But I may say before God and
you, that of all the events of my life, inclusive
of its afflictions, nothing has humbled me so
much as your love. Right or wrong it may be,
but true it is, and I tell you. Your love has
been to me like God's own love, which makes
the receivers of it kneelers.

Robert Browning to Elizabeth Barrett

Let me count my gold now—and rub off any
speck that stays the full shining. . . . I am yours
forever . . . I have your memory, the knowledge of you, the idea of you printed into my
heart and brain,—on that, I can live my life—
but it is for you, the dear, utterly generous
creature I know you, to give me more and
more beyond mere life—to extend life and
deepen it—as you do, and will do. Oh, how I
love you when I think of the entire truthful-
ness of your generosity to me—how, meaning
and willing to give, you gave nobly! Do you
think I have not seen in this world how women who *do* love will manage to confer that

gift on occasion? And shall I allow myself to fancy how much alloy such pure gold as *your* love would have rendered endurable? Yet it came, virgin ore, to complete my fortune! And what but this makes me confident and happy? . . . I am yours forever . . . .

Mary Wollstonecraft to Shelley

And where are you? and what are you doing, my blessed love; I hope and trust that for *my* sake you did not go outside this wretched day, while the wind howls and the clouds seem to threaten rain. And what did my love think of as he rode along—Did he think about our home, our babe and his poor Pecksie? But I am sure you did and thought of them all with joy and hope. But in the choice of residence— dear Shelley—pray be not too quick or attach yourself too much to one spot—Ah—were you indeed a winged Elf and could soar over mountains & seas and could pounce on the little spot—A house with a lawn, a river or lake— noble trees & divine mountains that should be our little mousehole to retire to. But never mind this—give me a garden . . . and I will thank my love for many favours.

PERCY BYSSHE SHELLEY,
English poet, from a contemporary portrait.

Lord Byron to Countess Guiccioli

I have read this book in your garden;—my
love, you were absent, or else I could not have
read it. It is a favorite book of yours, and the
writer was a friend of mine. You will not
understand these English words, and *others*
will not understand them,—which is the reason I have not scrawled them in Italian. But

you will recognize the handwriting of him who passionately loved you, and you will divine that, over a book which was yours, he could only think of love.

In that word, beautiful in all languages, but most so in yours—*Amor mio*—is comprised my existence here and hereafter. I feel I exist here, and I feel that I shall exist hereafter,— to *what* purpose you will decide; my destiny rests with you, and you are a woman, eighteen years of age, and two out of a convent, I wish that you had staid there, with all my heart,—

*Hand-painted German love note
with floral decoration.*

or, at least, that I had never met you in your married state.

But all this is too late. I love you, and you love me,—at least, you *say* so, and *act* as if you *did* so, which last is a great consolation in all events. But *I* more than love you, and cannot cease to love you.

Think of me, sometimes, when the Alps and ocean divide us,—but they never will, unless you *wish* it.

Beethoven to His Immortal Beloved

Though still in bed my thoughts go out to you, my Immortal Beloved, now and then joyfully, then sadly, waiting to learn whether or not fate will hear us. I can live only wholly with you or not at all—yes, I am resolved to wander so long away from you until I can fly to your arms and say that I am really at home, send my soul enwrapped in you into the land of spirits.—Yes, unhappily it must be so—you will be the more resolved since you know my fidelity—to you, no one can ever again possess my heart—none—never—Oh, God! why is it necessary to part from one whom one loves and yet my life in Vienna is now a wretched life—your love makes me at once the happiest and the unhappiest of men . . . Love me—today—yesterday—what tearful longings for you—you—you—my life—my all —farewell—Oh continue to love me—never misjudge the most faithful heart of your beloved L.

Victor Hugo to Adele Foucher

I wrote you a long letter, Adele, but it was too sad; I tore it up. I wrote it because you are the only creature in the world to whom I can speak freely of all I suffer and of all I fear. But perhaps it might have given you some pain, and I will never voluntarily make you suffer by my troubles. Besides, I forget them at once when we meet. You do not know—you cannot imagine—how great my happiness is when I see you, hear you speak, and feel you near me! Now that I have not seen you for two days, I think of it with an excitement that seems almost convulsive. When I have passed a few moments beside you I feel much better. There is something in your very glance, so noble and so generous, that seems to exalt me. When your eyes meet mine, it is as if your soul passed into me. And then—oh, then! my beloved Adele, I feel capable of accomplishing anything; I am strengthened by being endowed with all your gentle virtues.

How much I wish that you could read all that there is within me; that your soul could be infused into mine, as your smile infuses itself into my whole being! If we could be alone together, just for one hour, Adele. . . .

Lord Nelson to Fanny Nesbit

To write letters to you is the next greatest pleasure I feel to receiving them from you. What I experience when I read such as I am sure are the pure sentiments of your heart, my poor pen cannot express, nor indeed would I give much for any pen or head that could describe feelings of that kind; they are worth but little when that can happen. My heart yearns to you—it is with you; my mind dwells upon naught else but you. Absent from you, I feel no pleasure; it is you, my dearest Fanny, who are everything to me. Without you, I care not for this world, for I have found lately nothing in it but vexation and trouble.

These, you are well convinced, are my present sentiments; God Almighty grant they may never change. Nor do I think they will; indeed there is, as far as any human knowledge can judge, a moral certainty they cannot; for it must be real affection that brings us together, not interest or compulsion which makes so many unhappy . . . .

Dorothy Osborne to Sir William Temple

You needed not have feared that I should take occasion from your not answering my last not to write this week. You are as much pleased, you say, with writing to me as I can be to receive your letters. Why should you not think the same of me? In earnest you may, and if you love me you will, but then how much more satisfied should I be if there were no need of these and we might talk all that we write and more. Shall we ever be so happy?

Last night I was in the garden till 11 o'clock. It was the sweetest night that e'er I saw. The garden looked so well and the jasmine smelt beyond all perfume. And yet I was not pleased. The place had all the charms it used to have when I was most satisfied with it, and had you been there I should have liked it much more than ever I did; but that not being, it was no more to me than the next field, and only served me for a place to roam in without disturbance.

Jane Welsh to Thomas Carlyle

Unkind that you are ever to suffer me to be cast down, when it is so easy a thing for you to lift me to the Seventh Heaven! My soul was darker than midnight, when your pen said "let there be light," and there was light as at the bidding of the Word . . . Oh, my dearest Friend! be always so good to me, and I shall

*Hand-colored miniatures
often decorated envelopes and letters.*

make the best and happiest Wife. When I read in your looks and words that you love me, I feel it in the deepest part of my soul; then I care not one straw for the whole Universe beside.

Thomas Carlyle to Jane Welsh

Dear little Child! How is it that I have deserved thee; deserved a purer and nobler heart than falls to the lot of millions? I swear I will love thee with my whole heart, and think my life well spent if it can make thine happy.

. . . Let us pray to God that our holy purposes be not frustrated; let us trust in Him and in each other, and fear no evil that can befall us. My last blessing as a Lover is with you; this is my last letter to Jane Welsh: my first blessing as a Husband, my first kiss to Jane Carlyle is at hand! O my Darling! I will always love thee.

Robert Burns to Agnes M°Lehose

Clarinda, my life, you have wounded my soul. —Can I think of your being unhappy, even tho' it be not described in your pathetic elegance of language, without being miserable? Clarinda, can I bear to be told from you, that "you will not see me tomorrow night—that you wish the hour of parting were come"! Do not let us impose on ourselves by sounds: if in the moment of fond endearment and tender dalliance, I perhaps trespassed against the letter of Decorum's law; I appeal, even to you, whether I ever sinned in the very least degree against the spirit of her strictest statute.—But why, My Love, talk to me in such strong terms; every word of which cuts me to the very soul . . . ?

O Love and Sensibility, ye have conspired against My Peace! I love to madness, and I feel to torture! Clarinda, how can I forgive myself that I have ever touched a single chord in your bosom with pain! Would I do it willingly? Would any consideration, any gratification make me do so? O, did you love like me, you would not, you could not, deny or put off a meeting with the Man who adores you; who would die a thousand deaths before he would injure you; and who must soon bid you a long farewell!

Victor Hugo to Adele Foucher

. . . When two souls, which for a longer or a shorter time have sought each other amidst the crowd, at length find each other; when they perceive that they belong to each other; when, in short, they comprehend their affinity, then there is established between them a union, pure and ardent as themselves, a union begun upon earth in order that it may be completed in heaven. This union is *love*; real and perfect love, such love as very few men can adequately conceive; love which is a religion, adoring the being beloved as a divinity; love that lives in devotion and ardor, and for which to make great sacrifices is the purest pleasure. . . . Such love I have described to you is exclusive. I myself wish for nothing, not even a glance, from any other woman in the world; but I desire that no man should dare to claim anything from the woman who is mine. If I desire her alone, it is because I wish for her wholly and entirely. *. . . Adieu*

George Sand Tells of Her Stay With Chopin on Majorca

. . . So we bought the furniture for three times its value and we moved into the monastery of Valdemosa. It is a poetic name and a poetic dwelling; the landscape is wonderful, both wild and grandiose, the bow of the sea spreading across the horizon and awe-inspiring peaks close around us, and there are eagles pursuing their prey down to the very orange trees of our garden; a cypress avenue winds from the very top of our mountain into the depths of the gorge; there are cascades half hidden in myrtles and palm trees growing far below; no, nothing could have been more magnificent than our sojourn here!

FREDERICK CHOPIN,
from a painting by Delacroix in the Louvre, Paris.

Chopin Writes of His Beloved

I have, perhaps to my own misfortune, found my ideal; I revere her with all my soul. For six months now I have dreamed of her every night, and I have not yet advanced the first word. It was in thinking of this pure creature that I composed the adagio of my Concerto, as well as the waltz written just this morning which I mailed to you. Oh! how sad having no one with whom to share one's sorrows and joys! What bitterness when the oppressed heart is not able to unburden itself in the heart of another!

Bismarck to Johanna

Weep not, my angel; let your sympathy be strong and full of confidence in God; give him real consolation with encouragement, not with tears, and, if you can, doubly, for yourself and for your thankless friend whose heart is just now filled with you and has room for nothing else. Are you a withered leaf, a faded garment? I will see whether my love can foster the verdure once more, can brighten up the colors. You must put forth fresh leaves, and the old

ones I shall lay between the pages of the book of my heart so that we may find them when we read there, as tokens of fond recollection. You have fanned to life again the coal that under ashes and debris still glowed in me; it shall envelop you in life-giving flames.

In 19th century morning dress,
a lady opens a love letter.

Mary Wollstonecraft to Shelley

Goodnight, my love—tomorrow I will seal this blessing on your lips. Dear good creature, press me to you and hug your own Mary to your heart. Perhaps she will one day have a father —till then be every thing to me, my love—& indeed I will be a good girl and never vex you any more. I will learn Greek and—but when shall we meet when I may tell you all this & you will so sweetly reward me—oh we must meet soon for this is a dreary life. I am weary of it—a poor widowed deserted thing. No one cares for her—but—ah love, is not that enough —indeed I have a very sincere affection for my own Shelley—

But Goodnight, I am woefully tired & so

sleepy—I shall dream of you ten to one when, naughty one, you have quite forgotten me—

Take me—one kiss—well that is enough—tomorrow.

George Washington to His Wife, Martha

I am now set down to write you on a subject which fills me with inexpressable concern, and this concern is greatly aggravated and increased, when I reflect upon the uneasiness I know it will cause you. It has been determined in Congress that the whole army raised for the defense of the American cause shall be put under my care, and that it is necessary for me to proceed immediately to Boston to take upon me the command of it.

You may believe me, my dear Patsy [*a pet name*] when I assure you in the most solemn manner that, so far from seeking this appointment, I have used every endeavor in my power to avoid it, not only from my unwillingness to part from you and the family, but from a consciousness of its being a trust too great for my capacity, and that I should enjoy more real happiness in one month with you at home than I have the more distant prospect of finding

GEORGE AND MARTHA WASHINGTON,
in an old engraving.

55

abroad, if my stay were to be seven times seven years. But as it has been a kind of destiny which has thrown me upon this service, I shall hope that my undertaking it is designed to answer some good purpose. You might, and I suppose did, perceive, from the tenor of my letters, that I was apprehensive I could not avoid this appointment, as I did not pretend to intimate when I should return. That was the case. It was utterly out of my power to refuse this appointment, without exposing my character to such censure as would have reflected dishonor upon myself, and have given pain to my friends. This, I am sure, could not, and ought not to be pleasing to you, and must have lessened me considerably in my own esteem . . . . I shall rely, therefore, confidently on the Providence which has heretofore preserved and been bountiful to me, not doubting that I shall return safe to you in the fall . . . .

Richard Wagner to Minna Planer

It is only twenty-four hours since we parted, but I am lost in my misery and tears, and I can find joy in nothing, nothing whatever! You have become so very dear to me, you dear and

56

lovely child! How can I become accustomed to our separation so soon? How can I bear your absence? You have become part of me; without you in all my limbs it is as if a part of me were missing. Alas, if you felt only half my longing, then you, too, would be filled with love and memories. I continued to weep after you had gone. Tell me, were you angry about the letter I sent so late? Oh, I would almost have come to you myself, but then I knew I would have stayed with you and would have given up my journey and everything. Alas, who could describe my state of loneliness? Yes, my Minna, I love you and I am a little vain about it; you see, I imagine I have instilled life and soul into you which you didn't have before, so far as I knew. Besides, I often thought you didn't love me, but now I believe you do. Nay, when I gave you the last kiss, all your love overwhelmed twice and a thousand-fold. O my Life, don't forget, don't betray me ever, cling to me faithfully, remain my Minna, and if you ever felt love, so give it all to me and never let me share it with anyone else. Never forget that my whole heart is yours. Do you hear? Do you hear? Don't ever betray me! I now hate Leipzig and Magdeburg and everything. It is only you I love. Oh, join me soon so that I can see you and be convinced you love me still. Write by return mail if you still love me and still think of me. Write, write, and strengthen me, my angel. Soon, soon! Adieu! Adieu! Think of me, think of your Richard.

John Keats to Fanny Brawne

Your letter gave me more delight, than anything in the world but yourself could do; indeed I am almost astonished that any absent one should have that luxurious power over my senses which I feel. Even when I am not thinking of you I receive your influence and a tenderer nature stealing upon me. All my thoughts, my unhappiest days and nights, have I find not at all cured me of my love of Beauty, but made it so intense that I am miserable that you are not with me: or rather breathe in that dull sort of patience that cannot be called Life. I never knew before, what such a love as you have made me feel, was; I did not believe in it; my Fancy was afraid of it, lest it should burn me up. But if you will fully love me, though there may be some fire, 'twill not be more than we can bear when moistened and bedewed with Pleasures.

Heloise to Abelard

I have your picture in my room; I never pass it without stopping to look at it; and yet when you are present with me I scarce ever cast my eyes on it. If a picture, which is but a mute representation of an object, can give such pleasure, what cannot letters inspire? They have souls; they can speak; they have in them all that force which expresses the transports of the heart; they have all the fire of our passions, they can raise them as much as if the persons themselves were present; they have all the tenderness and the delicacy of speech, and sometimes even a boldness of expression beyond it.

Additional Biographical Notes

ABELARD *(1079-1142), medieval French theologian.*

LUDWIG VAN BEETHOVEN *(1770-1827).*

OTTO VON BISMARCK *(1815-1898).*

NAPOLEON BONAPARTE *(1769-1821), Emperor of France.*

ROBERT *(1812-1899), and* ELIZABETH BARRETT BROWNING *(1806-1861), English poets.*

ROBERT BURNS *(1759-1796).*

THOMAS CARLYLE *(1795-1881), Scottish essayist and historian.*

GIOVANNI JACOPO CASANOVA *(1725-1798).*

JOHN JAY CHAPMAN *(1862-1933), American essayist.*

FREDERICK CHOPIN *(1810-1849).*

SAMUEL TAYLOR COLERIDGE *(1772-1834), English poet and critic.*

MADAME DU BARRY *(1746-1793).*

GEORGE GORDON, LORD BYRON *(1788-1824).*

ALEXANDER HAMILTON *(1755-1804), American lawyer and statesman.*

HELOISE *(?-1164).*

HENRY VIII, *(1491-1547).*

VICTOR HUGO *(1802-1885), French novelist.*

JOSEPHINE *(1763-1814).*

JOHN KEATS *(1795-1821), English poet.*

LOUIS XV *of France (1710-1774).*

60

LORD HORATIO NELSON *(1758-1821)*,
   British naval hero.
GEORGE SAND *(1803-1876), pseudonym of*
   French writer Baronne Dudevant.
PERCY BYSSHE SHELLEY *(1792-1822).*
SIR RICHARD STEELE *(1672-1729), British*
   essayist and dramatist.
SIR WILLIAM TEMPLE *(1628-1699), English*
   diplomat, statesman and essayist.
WILLIAM MAKEPEACE THACKERAY *(1811-1863)*,
   English novelist.
JAMES THOMSON *(1700-1748), Scottish poet.*
VOLTAIRE *(1694-1778), French writer,*
   satirist and philosopher.
RICHARD WAGNER *(1813-1883).*
GEORGE WASHINGTON *(1732-1799), first*
   President of the United States.

My Beloved

Designed by Harald Peter.
Set in Monotype Walbaum, a light, open typeface
designed by Justus Erich Walbaum (1768-1839),
who was a type founder at Goslar and at Weimar.
Printed on Hallmark Eggshell Book paper.